MEET THE SAINTS

Four tongue-in-cheek sketches about our Patron Saints

by
Margaret Franks

MOORLEY'S Print & Publishing

British Library Cataloguing in Publication Data.
A catalogue record for this book is available
from the British Library.

ISBN 0 86071 538 8

MOORLEY'S Print & Publishing
23 Park Rd., Ilkeston, Derbys DE7 5DA
Tel/Fax: (0115) 932 0643

CONTENTS

Dewi and the Dragon

A play for St David's Day
March 1st

Cast:

> 1st Narrator
> 2nd Narrator
> Dragon
> 1st Job applicant
> 2nd Job applicant
> 3rd Job applicant
> (Other applicants may swell the queue)
> Dewi Sant
> Dove

Dewi Sant or St David is one of our home grown patron saints, and as such we have a lot of information about him. But as to why the Welsh flag bears a red dragon, we can only speculate, which is one of the reasons this playlet was written. The other reason is to emphasise the real Dewi Sant, his commitment to Jesus and his Christian love and compassion for others.

1st Narrator: This is a true -

2nd Narrator: made up story!

1st Narrator: Many, many years ago -

2nd Narrator: long before the very first Rugby match -

1st Narrator: in the wildest part of wild Wales -

2nd Narrator: somewhere off the A40 -

1st Narrator: amidst the swirling mists and driving rain -

2nd Narrator: of the wettest part of wild Wales -

1st Narrator:	there was heard a terrible wailing! Wail after wail after wail!
2nd Narrator:	Which is why it is called Wales, if you've ever wondered!
1st Narrator:	Wailing AND weeping! Sound effects please! *(Off-stage wailing and weeping noises)* And who should appear but – A DRAGON! *(Enter smallish ruddy dragon)*
2nd Narrator:	AHH! (Hides behind 1st N.)
1st Narrator:	There's nothing to be scared of! It's only a myth.
2nd Narrator:	What's a myth?
1st Narrator:	Like this, a true made-up story.
2nd Narrator:	*(Reluctantly re-appearing)* Well, a myth is as good as a mile as far as I'm concerned.
1st Narrator:	This dragon. Well, it was like nothing else in heaven or earth! Its neck was covered in scales like a fish! All four legs were scaled and ended in terrible claws. *(Dragon mimes all these attributes).* Its back was scaled and its tongue was barbed! The wings of the dragon were like those of a giant bat and its tail was long and writhing, ending in a huge, vicious barb!
2nd Narrator:	I'm glad it's only a myth!
1st Narrator:	And it was this unearthly creature that was wailing and weeping.
Dragon:	Boo Hoo!!!
2nd Narrator:	Why?
Dragon:	Because I've been abandoned in a strange wild land.

Narrators:	Ah!
1st Narrator:	Who abandoned you?
2nd Narrator:	And how did you get here in the first place?
Dragon:	It is a long story -
2nd Narrator:	I knew it!
Dragon:	But I'll tell you anyway. It was the Romans who brought me. When they conquered Britain they brought me on their shields! I was riding high then I can tell you! All the wild natives bowed down to me. It was the best time of my life. Then the Romans left – in a hurry.
1st Narrator:	Ah, I know what's coming. When you have to pack up and leave in a hurry, something always gets left behind.
2nd Narrator:	- keys, passports, spare underpants -
Dragon:	*(Sadly)* and dragons! They simply forgot me. And now I'm doomed to wander this wild wet land alone and with no friend. I haven't talked to a soul for over a hundred years.
2nd Narrator:	Why not?
Dragon:	I only speak Latin, I don't understand Welsh!
1st Narrator:	Couldn't you have made a few friends by lighting the kitchen fires with your - you know- fiery breath?
Dragon:	Well, you know about all this rain?
2nd Narrator:	Put your fire out did it? *(Dragon nods)*
1st Narrator:	Dear me. Still, no doubt you've fed well on plenty of plump Welsh people?

Dragon:	You are joking! I was brought up on spaghetti and olives! I'm strictly vegetarian!
2nd Narrator:	Bad luck.
Dragon:	So I'm doomed to wander in this wild land, hungry, homeless and unloved. Wail! Wail! Wail!
1st Narrator:	Just a minute. Don't despair. *(To 2nd Narrator)* You know, that gives me an idea!
2nd Narrator:	I was waiting for that!
1st Narrator:	Who are those people who are supposed to look after the homeless, the hungry and the poor unloved of this world?
2nd Narrator:	I'm with you! You mean the Christians!
Dragon:	The Christians? Who are they?
1st Narrator:	They came after the Romans. And if I'm not much mistaken some of them live very near here. It's a monastery run by a man called Dewi Sant. He's got quite a reputation around here. In fact if you join this queue of people here you'll learn all about him and what the Christians do! *(Enter a queue of applicants for Dewi's monastery)*
2nd Narrator:	Are you sure this is a good idea?
1st Narrator:	Have you got a better one? No? Well just listen in. *(Dragon joins back of queue. All the people in the queue are grumbling).*
1st Applicant:	How long have you been here?
2nd Applicant:	Too long! At least a week.
3rd Applicant:	You're lucky, I've been here over nine days!
1st Applicant:	Why does he keep us waiting so long?

8

3rd Applicant: It's a kind of test. You know, do we really want the job.

1st Applicant: I'm beginning to wonder.

2nd Applicant: Why did you come?

1st Applicant: I read the advertisement. *(Gets out a piece of paper and reads from it.)*
Wanted!
Monks for Dewi Sant's monastery.
Do you want a purpose in life?
A secure job – for life?
Fantastic rewards?
No previous experience necessary,
Just apply to Dewi Sant's Monastery
Mynyw,
Wild wet Wales.
Please form an orderly queue outside main gate.

2nd Applicant: A job for life! That can't be bad.

3rd Applicant: I like the bit about fantastic rewards.

1st Applicant: But what's he like, this Dewi?

2nd Applicant: Oh, an amazing bloke!

3rd Applicant: Does miracles, you know.

1st Applicant: Tell me.

3rd Applicant: Well, he was preaching to these people in his cardigan –

2nd Applicant: No! At Cardigan, not in his cardigan.

3rd Applicant: Sorry! Well not every one could see or hear him, so all of a sudden underneath his feet, the earth rose up and he was standing on a hill, so they could all see him and hear what he was saying.

2nd Narrator: Are they troubled with moles in Wales?

1st Narrator: Be quiet!

3rd Applicant: AND... a white dove settled on his shoulder, just like it happened to you know who.

1st Applicant: Who?

2nd Applicant: Who?

3rd Applicant: That's right. Hoo hoo! A dove.

2nd Narrator: That is a terrible joke.

1st Narrator: You have to suffer for your faith!

3rd Applicant: Look out! Here he comes now!
(Dewi Sant enters with dove. Everyone cheers)

All: Dewi Sant! Dewi Sant! Hooray! etc.

Dewi: Blessings on you all. I am Dewi Sant and this is my dove.

Dove: Coo!

Dewi: I see we have the usual bunch of hopefuls wanting to join the order.

All Applicants: Yes please!

Dewi: Well, let me tell you something about our life here. We have given ourselves God and we follow his son Jesus who loved us and showed us the way to love others.

1st Applicant: Sounds wonderful.

Dewi: And to serve him properly these are some of the things we do.

First; we hardly ever speak to anyone, unless it is absolutely necessary, for example "Please remove your candle, it has set fire to my habit."

(As he speaks the applicants begin to look worried and disconcerted)

Secondly, When we do speak it is in Latin. And you will have to learn ALL of the psalms in the Bible in Latin off by heart.

Thirdly, we work very hard to support ourselves on our farm, but we do not even allow ourselves oxen, we have to pull the plough ourselves.

1st Applicant: Gosh, all that hard work will make you hungry, I expect you eat well?

Dewi: Oh, very well. We eat bread, salt and vegetables. Oh, and we can drink as much water as we like!

2nd Applicant: *(Shaking his head)* Oh, great!

3rd Applicant: What about – er – entertainment?

Dewi: Oh, we frequently enjoy ourselves praying all day standing up to our necks in cold water!

1st Applicant: Coo!

Dove: *(Angrily)* Coo!

Dewi: And of course, we are a little stern with ourselves at the weekend.

2nd Applicant: *(In disbelief)* A little stern…?

Dewi: Yes. We stay awake and in prayer from Friday evening until Sunday morning!

All Applicants: COO!

Dove: *(Angrily)* Coo! Coo!

1st Applicant:	But… what about all those fantastic rewards?
2nd Applicant:	Yes, tell us about those!
Dewi:	Well of course there are tremendous rewards! Doesn't it say in the Bible "and great will be your reward in Heaven"?
1st Applicant:	Er, thank you Dewi Sant, you have made everything clear. This is a very important decision I have to make. I must go away and think very carefully about it. Er, er yes… *(Leaves hurriedly)*
2nd Applicant:	Yes, I, er don't think I'm tall enough for the job. I'll go back to the job centre. *(Leaves)*
Dewi:	Oh dear, it's the same thing every time. What about you? Do you want to join?
3rd Applicant:	Er, I'd love to, really, it sounds great, but I er, need to settle one or two problems at home first. But I'll be back… probably… possibly… er yes… *(Leaves)*
Dewi:	*(To Dove)* There they go. No one left as usual.
Dove:	*(Sympathetically)* Coo!
Dragon:	Yes there is! I'm still here!
Dewi:	Good gracious! What have we here? Whatever are you?
Dragon:	I'm a mythical beast. A ruddy dragon!
Dewi:	I'm glad you said that.
Dragon:	*(With dignity)* I was referring to my colour. Ruddy gold!
Dewi:	I beg your pardon. But what can I do for you?
Dragon:	I want to join your order.

Dewi:	You do? After all you've heard?
Dove:	Coo!!
Dragon:	Oh, yes please! This place will suit me down to the ground.
Dewi:	But what about the conditions? We hardly ever speak.
Dragon:	I haven't spoken to anyone since 410 A.D.
Dewi:	And the Latin?
Dragon:	I speak it like a native! I <u>was</u> a native!
Dewi:	Wonderful. But how about the never ending toil?
Dragon:	Hard work doesn't frighten me. I could make the furrows with my barbed tail!
Dewi:	And the diet? Surely that will be impossible for you?
Dragon:	Not at all. I was raised a vegetarian. You name the vegetable – I'll eat it. I'm very partial to leek soup by the way.
Dewi:	*(Thoughtfully)* Leeks? Now that's an idea.
Dragon:	And as for staying awake from Friday to Sunday morning, well, dragons never sleep anyway!
Dewi:	Ah, but what about prayer? Do you know what that is?
Dragon:	Does prayer mean getting in touch with the one you follow? The one who wants you to look after the homeless and the hungry?
Dewi:	Absolutely.

Dragon:	Then that's no problem. I shall learn fast. And as for standing around in cold water, my fishy scales are made for it! Will you have me, Dewi Sant?
Dewi:	With all my heart! Welcome Brother Dragon! Wales will be proud of you! *(Gives the dragon a big hug)*
1st Narrator:	There you are! Happy endings all round!
2nd Narrator:	And it's true?
1st Narrator:	Of course, I made it up myself only last week. The true, new, made up, legend of Dewi and the dragon!
Dove:	*(Angrily)* Coo! Coo!
1st Narrator:	Oh, sorry! The legend of Dewi, the Dove and the Dragon!

The End

George and the Job Application

A play for St George's Day
April 23rd

Cast:
Chair Angel
Recording Angel
Angel
George

There seems to be little we know about St George apart from the fact that he was martyred for the faith by the Emperor Diocletian in AD 303. Everything else was added long after and for reasons we can only guess at. Does that mean we really only love him for his dragon?

Scene: *A longish table behind which are three chairs, the middle one slightly more imposing than the others. There is a pile of papers before each chair.*
There is a further chair in front of the table to the right at an angle.
Enter three angels, one obviously the Chairangel, the second the Recording angel (more secretarial), the third angel – just an angel.
They sit down at the table and start shuffling the papers about.

Chair: *(Exasperated)* This job is taking longer than I expected.

Recording: We've had thousands of applicants.   Some of them most unsuitable.

Chair: Perhaps we haven't made it clear what is really required.   Read the job advertisement again.

Recording: *(Reading from a paper)*
SPECIAL ANNOUNCEMENT
The Angelic Council for Patron Saints wishes it known that there is a position, FOR THE RIGHT PERSON, as Patron Saint for the kingdom of ENGLAND, part of the British Isles,

15

North west of the European Continent. Climate, chilly and damp, peopled by a mongrel race of limited intellectual ability. No previous experience necessary.
Martyrdom not essential, but preferred.

Angel: I can't see the attraction myself.

Chair: *(Shocked)* What? Patron Saint? Think of the prestige.

Angel: Yes.. but... patron saint of England?

Chair: *(Thoughtfully)* Er, yes, I see what you mean. Still it is an honour. And think of the perks.

Angel: Such as?

Chair: Well... there's your face on all the bank notes... a whole day devoted to your name... and ... er...

Recording: And your example and witness!

Chair: What? Oh, well, that too I suppose.

Recording: How about seeing this one next? Candidate 3085. Name of George.

Angel: George... George, yes that has a ring about it.

Chair: *(Enthusiastically)* Yes, short and manly. The sort of name that people can shout for when going to battle!

Recording: *(Severely)* I'm not sure I approve of that.

Chair: Oh, you are an old pacifist! People like fighting, especially the English.

Recording: You can say that again. We've only just weaned the bloodthirsty Anglo-Saxons off worshipping Woden!

Angel: George... George... I've heard the name somewhere before. Something about...

Chair:	It's a pity we're so short staffed. We could have got through this list ages ago if only Michael had spared the time to help us.
Recording:	Oh, I don't know. I think we're better off without the archangel. He can be a bit of a dragon at times.
Angel:	Dragon! That's it! Something about a dragon! I knew I'd heard the name before.
Chair:	George? George and the dragon? He's not the one who…
Angel:	*(Excitedly)* Yes! Cappodocia, Lybia and the king's daughter. Oh, it's very romantic.
Chair:	AND very good PR! Let's have him in.
Recording:	Wait a minute. There's nothing in his application form about dragons.
Angel:	*(Dashed)* Oh. Oh, well, perhaps he's just modest and doesn't like to boast.
Chair:	Could it be another George? That could be awkward. How can we find out?
Recording:	Ask him.
Chair:	That might be difficult. We don't want to embarrass him.
Angel:	Leave it to me. I'll ask some leading questions. We'll worm it out of him. *(Giggles).* Get it? Worm it out of him? Dragons were known as great worms.
Recording:	*(Coldly, getting up and walking out right)* I haven't had your education.
Chair:	Of course, he would be just the man for the job. Dragon-killer! The English would love that. *Recording angel comes back leading George who stands in front of the table.*
Chair:	Good morning, applicant 3085.

George:	*(He has a military "officer class" air about him. He stands to attention)* Good morning sir!
Chair:	Welcome to the interviewing committee. I'm sorry you've been kept waiting so long.
George:	Not to worry! Used to sitting around waiting for orders, don't you know!
Chair:	Er, yes, of course. Do take a seat.
George:	Thank you sir. *(Sits down on chair in front)*
Chair:	Good, then let's begin by checking some of the details on your application form. Name?
George:	George.
Chair:	Profession?
George:	Soldier.
Chair:	Splendid. Place of birth?
George:	Dipolis, Palestine.
Recording:	*(Leaning over confidentially)* That's modern Lydda you know.
Chair:	I know! Now, er, George, date of birth?
George:	Third century do?
Chair:	Yes, we don't bother too much with details like that. Now, your career.
George:	Martyred for the faith in AD 303, seen at the battle of Antioch encouraging the crusaders AD 1098.
Chair:	Splendid. Do you have proof of your martyrdom?
George:	Yes sir. A signed affidavit from the executioner. *(Hands over paper)*.
Chair:	Well that seems to be in order... Now -

Angel:	*(Butting in)* Hobbies?
George:	Sir?
Angel:	Er, any hobbies, you know, interests that take up your spare time?
George:	Ah, yes! *(Enthusiastically)* Horses!
Angel:	*(Brightening up)* Oh, you like animals?
George:	Well yes, horses you know. Wonderful creatures, bless 'em.
Angel:	*(Fishing)* No... er other pets? Like... er... birds?
George:	*(Puzzled)* Er... no. No Birds.
Angel:	No.. er.. reptiles?
George:	Reptiles??!!
Angel:	Yes, you know, frogs, tadpoles. No tadpoles? Er... lizards, er ..worms?
Recording:	*(Exasperated) He* means dragons! Do you keep dragons?
Chair:	No, no, no. Do you <u>fight</u> dragons? Or did you ever fight dragons? I mean, are you the George that fought and killed the dragon?
George:	Ah. I see. I was afraid of this.
Chair:	Well, are you?
George:	Yes.
Chair:	*(Pleased)* Ah!
George:	And no.
Chair:	What?
George:	Only sort of.
Chair:	I beg your pardon?

George:	You see, well, this is very embarrassing, you see, there never was a dragon.
Angel:	No dragon?
George: Recording:	But I'm the George that is supposed to have killed it. You're the George that killed the dragon, only you didn't because there wasn't one. It's perfectly clear.
Chair:	*(Unhappily)* But I don't see…
George:	Made up.
Chair:	What was?
George:	The story. Of the dragon.
Chair:	You made it up?
George:	No, no! Followers you know. *(Modestly)* Got a bit of a fan club. They made it up.
Angel:	Why?
George:	Well, makes a good story, don't you know, something to tell the children around the fire on a long winter's night.
Recording:	But why you?
George:	Well, bit of a dull old stick, you see, just an old soldier and they like their heroes more dashing and exciting.
Chair:	Who do?
George:	The ladies, bless 'em. And the chaps. Ask the crusaders. They're the ones that talked me into applying for the job. Wouldn't take no for an answer. Seemed to think I'd been helpful in the Holy Land. Trouble is, the story stuck. I did try to shake it off. No go. George must have his dragon. Even though it isn't true. Sorry to disappoint you and all that.

There is a pause while they all look at him silently.

Chair: *(Regretfully)* No dragon.

George: *(With a sad finality)* No, no dragon. *(Pause)*
              Well, there it is, I suppose I'd better be taking my leave. *(Gets up to go).*

Recording: Hang on a moment! *(Stands up hands on hips)* Just let me ask you one question.

George: *(Standing to attention)* Sir!

Recording: Why were you martyred?

George: Ah, that. Well, couldn't let the captain down.

Chair: The captain?

George: Jesus. The Boss. My company commander. Couldn't let him down, could I?

Recording: So you died because you wouldn't give up your faith in Jesus.

George: Well, he was the best thing that ever happened to this old soldier. He died for me. Only fair I died for Him.

Recording: I see. Would you mind waiting over there for a minute?

George: Certainly sir. *(Goes over to side right)*

Recording: *(Turns to the other two)* What are we playing at?

Chair: What do you mean?

Recording: What are we playing at, worrying about a silly fairy story and disappointed there was no dragon? That man died for his faith. He loved his Lord so much he gave his life for him. He's the ideal candidate. Loyal, committed, brave – why the man's a saint!

Chair: You're right! He is a pretty good chap; honest, straight -

Angel: Loves animals -

Chair: Modest -

21

Angel: Unassuming -

Chair: Decent -

Angel: Fair-minded -

Chair: Thoroughly -

Angel: Thoroughly -

Both: ENGLISH!

Recording: *(Dryly)* Or what they ought to be! What an example he will be for them.

Chair: Even without the dragon.

Recording: *(Sitting down)* Oh, I don't think you're going to get rid of the dragon.

Angel: Don't be silly. There was no dragon.

Recording: No one is going to believe that. I am afraid he's stuck with it.

Chair: Come to think of it, they'll love that dragon. They're not a very imaginative bunch and they'll use it as a metaphor for centuries for all the things they detest, like unfairness, cheating at cards, income tax –

Recording: And foreigners!

Angel: Well, George will have to work on that one. After all he's a foreigner himself.

Chair: And think of all the hymns they can write – "'gainst the dragons of anger, the ogres of greed,"!

Angel: That's very good.

Chair: *(Modestly)* Yes, it's a good line isn't it. I'll have to get someone to write it.

Recording: Well?

22

Chair: Well what?

Recording: Does he get the job?

Chair: *(Rising)* Well, of course he does! He's the ideal man. I spotted
            that the minute he walked in. Are we all agreed?

Other two: Absolutely!

Chair: Er, George? Would you come back here for a moment please?

George: *(Returning)* Certainly Sir!

Chair: It gives me great pleasure to tell you that it is our unanimous
            decision to offer you the position of Patron Saint of England!
            You are obviously the best man for the job. Congratulations!

George: Thank you, sir!

Chair: Welcome aboard! *(All three shake his hand.)*

George: Thank you very much, sir. Those crusader chaps will be pleased.
            Of course you do realise I can only do the job part time?

Chair: *(Scandalised)* Part time??!

George: Yes, you see I'm already patron saint of the Italian Cavalry.

Angel: *(Faintly)* Of course – the horses!

George: And I help a couple of the chaps to look after Istanbul.

Chair: *(Fascinated)* You do?

George: Yes, so I have to spread myself around a bit. Still, it will be
            jolly nice to come here for the holidays.

Recording: Try Clacton!

George: Right, I will. Well, goodbye sirs, see you next when I report
            for duty! (He salutes, turns smartly and exits right.)

They look after him for a short pause then begin to gather up their papers.

Chair: Well, I think we managed that in a very satisfactory manner.

Angel: Absolutely. You know I think you're right. George will be an excellent name to take men into battle. Just think – *(Shouting)* "Cry God, for Harry, England and St. George!"

Chair: *(Leading him out left.)* Very inspiring. It will ring down the ages!

Recording: *(Disapprovingly)* Not if I get to Harry first! *(Follows them out.)*

The End

Patrick and the Producer

A play for St Patrick's Day
March 17th

Cast:

> Film Producer (F.P.)
> Producer's Assistant (Sam)
> Patrick
> Nennius

Patrick is our only other home grown Patron Saint, and so we have a great deal of information about him, amazingly from his own biography. Unfortunately this information is clogged up with so many romantic and sentimental embellishments, the real miracle of his mission to Ireland is often lost along with his tough uncompromising witness to the Lord. In fact we tend to think of him as just a quaint, folksy, Irish character – and he wasn't even Irish!

Enter harassed film producer talking into mobile phone. An equally harassed and even more worried assistant follows him round, up and down stage.

F. P.:   Joe? Get me the casting director! Why? I wanna blow his ear off!

Ass.:   F. P.? F.P.?

F. P.:   I don't care what he's doing. He could be painting himself green and sitting on the top of the Eiffel Tower for all I care! Just get him on the phone! *(To Assistant)* What is it? *(Into phone)* Don't go away! I haven't finished with you yet. *(To Ass.)* Now what?

Ass.:   F. P. The leprechauns have arrived!

F.P.:   At last. How many?

Ass.:   Five.

F. P.:   FIVE??!! What sort of a picture do you think we're making? How many leprechauns d'you think there are in Ireland? Spielberg'll be laughing his socks off! Get me fifty! *(Into phone)* Have you found him yet?

Ass.:   *(Despairingly)* F. P.! F. P.! We can't get fifty. We were lucky to get this number – and they all want double time!

F. P.:   Double Time???!!!

Ass.:   Well they say they don't usually work during the day, it's past their bedtime.

F. P.:   Well I'll be – *(Into phone)* What's that? You've got him? Good! Put him on! *(To Ass.)* Don't go away! Are we ready for the sea battle yet?

Ass.:   *(Unhappily)* Well…

F. P.:   WELL??!!

Ass.:   Well, the local water company hasn't agreed a figure yet for filling the tank, and… and the camera crews are still at lunch.

F. P.:   LUNCH?? Who said they could go to lunch??!!

Ass.:   You did F. P.

F. P.:   NONSENSE!! I never take lunch, why should they? *(Into phone)* Ah! There you are you son-of-a- What?! What do you mean what do I mean? You know what I mean! Where's my lead? Where's my star? A multi-million dollar production on the life of St Patrick and no star!! *(To Ass.)* What are you standing there for? Go and fill that tank! *(As Assistant runs off, shouts after him)* AND DON'T LOSE ANY LEPRECHAUNS! *(Into phone)* What? Leprechauns? Yeah, we got those – what there are of them! *(Listens a moment)* I don't care if you were up half the night looking for them! What d'you think I'm paying you for? Yes… yes…yes… I know! We got the pirates… yes… and the slaves…. and the dancing girls… AND the heavenly

26

choirs… yes - monks? Er… are they the guys in the dressing gowns? Oh, yeah, we got those… BUT WHERE'S MY LEAD??? WHERE'S ST PATRICK?

Ass.: *(Enters with clip board and papers)* F. P.? F. P.?

F. P.: Look! This is the biggest epic since – since – forever! You can forget about Ben Hur! You can forget about the Titanic! THIS is the one that's goin' to scoop the Oscars! But I must have a star! I MUST HAVE ST PATRICK!!!

Ass.: F. P.! He's here!!

F. P.: Do what?

Ass.: He's here, F. P.! St Patrick's here!

F. P.: Here? *(Into phone)* Hold everything! I think you've just saved your hide!! I'll call you back! *(Puts down phone ariel)* He's here! Great. Who's he sent us? Tom Cruise? Sean Connery? Silvester Stallone?

Ass.: No, F. P. you don't get it. HE is here. St Patrick himself.

F. P.: That's right, Sam, bring him in!

Assistant beckons off stage and two monks enter, one quite grizzled and elderly, the other young and bright-eyed.

F. P.: OH, no! NO! Not more monks *(to Ass.)* Get them out of here. Sorry fellas! We're full with monks.

Ass.: *(Despairingly)* You don't understand, F. P. This IS St Patrick! Himself! The REAL St Patrick! IN PERSON!

F. P.: The Real - ?? You don't say! Well I'll be - !! Of course! Our technical advisor! Say, am I pleased to meet you! *(Goes up to the young monk vigorously shakes him by the hand)* How do you do, Saint!

Ass.:	No, no, F. P. *(Points to older man)* THIS is St Patrick!
F. P.:	Oh, oh, er… of course *(Shakes his hand)* How do you do Saint? Of course an old… er… mature man like yourself – great life – er, glad to have you aboard!
Patrick:	Thank you.
F. P.:	May I say what a privilege it is to make a movie of your life?
Patrick:	It was a privilege to live it.
F. P.:	Oh, yeah, naturally, all that experience and … er … that. So you've come to see what a great job we're doing?
Patrick:	I believe I've come to put you straight about one or two things.
F. P.:	Believe me, Saint, you've got nothing to worry about. We've got the best, right down to the authentic leprechauns!
Patrick:	*(To Nennius the young monk)* Leprechauns? What are they?
Nennius:	I think they are magic fairy folk, Father Patrick, little spirits formerly believed in by the superstitious peasantry of Ireland.
Patrick:	That won't do at all!
F. P.	Who is this guy?
Patrick:	Allow me to introduce my young assistant Nennius.
F. P.:	Pleased to meet you young fella, but don't stick your oar in. Be like my assistant Sam here, just do as you're told! *(to Ass.)* How's the tank filling?
Ass.:	*(Nervously)* Halfway, F. P.
Nennius:	You mistake me, Sir, we don't wish to interfere, but as followers of Jesus Christ we don't believe in magic spirits.

F. P.:   *(Worried)* No spirits?

Patrick: Except of course the Holy Spirit.

F. P.:   *(Really puzzled)* Oh, right, the Holy Spirit! *(To Ass.)* Is he on the cast list? *(Ass. shrugs his shoulders nonplussed)*

Nennius: Father Patrick is referring to the third member of the Trinity.

F. P.:   The what?

Patrick: *(Firmly)* God the Father, God the Son and God the Holy Spirit! I can see you need a little more "technical" advice than you anticipated!

F. P.:   *(Uneasily)* Well, sure, Saint, we gotta be authentic. Er... er well, see to that Sam, will you?

Ass.:   *(Whispers in is ear)*

F. P.:   What? *(Smiling)* Oh, the shamrock! Why didn't you say?

Patrick: It's true, the shamrock is a useful illustration of the mystery of the Trinity.

F. P.:   *(Relieved)* Well, we got that right! But er.. say ..er Saint, sorry to mention it, but you don't sound... well, Irish?

Patrick: *(Calmly)* I'm not.

F. P.:   *(Staggered)* Not... not Irish??!!

Nennius: Father Patrick was born near the Clyde.

F. P.:   *(To Ass.)* Clyde? Clyde? As in Bonnie and - ?

Ass: No F. P. It's in the north of England.

F. P.:   *(Scandalised)* ENGLAND!!!! *(Horrified)* You're English?? How can I make an epic Irish movie about an Englishman?!! The New York police would never forgive me!!!

Patrick: Rest assured, young man, there were no English at the time of my birth. I was Roman British.

F. P.:   *(Bewildered)* Roman – *(To Ass.)* Look it up will you? Gee, Saint, you've sure thrown a spanner in the works! How do I know we've got the rest of it right? I'd better check it out straight off. You were captured by pirates?

Patrick: That is correct.

F. P.:   *(Sighing with relief)* Great! We keep the pirates. *(To Ass.)* How's the tank going?

Ass.:   Nearly full F. P.

F. P.   Great. *(Takes his clip board away)* Get those wasters out of lunch and start shooting.

Ass.:   Right away, F. P. *(Exits right)*

F. P.:   Now we're in business! Okay Saint, so next, you were a slave?

Patrick: Certainly. I served as a slave six long years among the pagan tribes of Ireland.

F. P.:   Gee, that's – dreadful. *(To himself, checking off list on clipboard)* Great! We get to keep the slaves.

Patrick: On the contrary, young man it was a blessed time.

F. P.:   It was???!!

Patrick: Oh it was. That time of exile and slavery – the long dark years were lit up by the love of Jesus. He had suffered and died for me – what were my hardships when he stood beside me? My faith grew and my spirit was lifted up to say a hundred prayers a day!

F. P.:   *(Unenthusiastically)* Great! Great.

Nennius: *(Enthusiastically and waving his arms about)* It was wonderful!
             Just like Joseph in Genesis! You know saying to his brothers
             "You meant it for evil, but God meant it for good!"

F. P.:   *(Searching his memory)* Genesis... Genesis... don't tell me...
             that was ... er.. *(Triumphantly)* Charlton Heston wasn't it?

Patrick: Then after six years I was warned in a dream to make my escape.

F. P.:   *(Brightening)* A dream? Great... a dream. *(Mutters to himself)*
             Good, good... a great dream sequence... we get to use the
             heavenly choir!

Nennius: Father Patrick ran away and travelled for two hundred miles to
             reach the shore and a ship he knew by faith was waiting for him.

F. P.:   Great! More sea battles!

Patrick: *(Dryly)* Only with the weather.

F. P.:   *(Hopefully)* Shipwreck?

Patrick: No, young man, we landed safely, but in a dreadful wilderness
             where there was no sustenance.

F. P.:   No Sus-?

Nennius: They had no food.   Father Patrick will make light of his
             sufferings but it was only by his faith and prayers that he and the
             sailors found sufficient to eat.

F. P.:   Good, good, starving sequence... miraculous food...

Patrick: Finally God led me home. but not for long. For there I heard the
             voices of the troubled people of Ireland, "We beseech you, you
             who are dedicated to God, come and walk among us once more!
             Bring us the Gospel of Jesus!"

31

Nennius: *(Enthusiastically)* Just like St Paul, you know! "Come over into Macedonia and help us!"

F. P.:   *(Struggling)* M-m-macedonia?

Patrick: Don't muddle the poor fellow! Just give thanks to God that after many years the Lord granted them according to their cry!

Nennius: But first Father Patrick went to France to study to become a priest.

F. P.:   *(Groaning)* Oh, no, not France! If we have the French in, that'll mean sub-titles!
             (St Patrick and Nennius look at each other in puzzlement, shrug their shoulders and shake their heads.)

F. P.:   Never mind! What happened next?

Patrick: The Church sent me back to Ireland where I laboured for God's kingdom for the rest of my life. His name be praised!

F. P.:   *(After a pause)* That's it?

Patrick: It?

F. P.:   That's all there is? Nothing else?

Patrick: What more do you want?

F. P.:   *(Pleadingly)* Well... didn't you do... weren't there any... you know... miracles?

Patrick: Oh, miracles! Plenty of those!

F. P.:   Great! For the moment there you had me worried.

Patrick: Miracles galore by the grace of God. Thousands renouncing their pagan ways and giving themselves to Jesus Christ wherever the Good News of his saving power was preached!

Nennius:	The whole island won for God!
F. P.:	*(Carefully)* Yeah... great... but... you know something a little more... er visual... er fights with the Druids? Er... no earthquakes?...Er... and what about the ... you know... the sn-

Enter Assistant shouting at the top of his voice...

Ass.:	SNAKES!!!!!
F. P.:	WHATT!!!!
Ass.:	F. P.! F. P.! The snakes have escaped!!!
Patrick:	*(With growing wrath)* SNAKES??
Nennius:	*(Nervously)* Now, now Father Patrick don't... don't...
F. P.:	What do you mean escaped???!!!
Ass:	They got out of their box when the trainer was at lunch!!!
F. P.:	*(Furious)* LUNCH?? Lunch was it?? I'll blow up that canteen before I'm through with this movie!!
Patrick:	*(Awfully)* WHAT SNAKES?
F. P.:	*(Quailing)* Well, you know, the snakes... your snakes... the snakes you got rid of -
Patrick:	*(In a full blown rage strides up and down in his fury with Nennius in tow ineffectually trying to calm him down and F. P. and the Assistant shrinking back every time he comes near).* THIS IS TOO MUCH! Am I never to hear the last of that foolishness? That tale told to children? Here I am, chancing death and disaster, out facing heathen tribes and their bloodthirsty chiefs - just for the sake of the Kingdom!!! And all I am remembered for is getting rid of a few poor harmless reptiles!

Nennius: Now, now, Father Patrick, please don't... don't... remember your age!

Patrick: SNAKES is it? I'll give them snakes! *(Shaking his fist at F.P. who hides behind his Assistant.)* I'LL GIVE YOU SNAKES!

Ass.:   Sss-sorry, your worship, your saintliness...

Patrick: *(Beginning to calm down but shaken)* Yes, well, perhaps I've been a bit hasty, it probably wasn't your fault young man...

F. P.:   *(Taking over again)* Sam!

Ass.:   Yes F. P.?

F. P.:   Get rid of the snakes! And don't make another mistake like that!

Ass.:   No. F. P.. Gosh I'm sorry... I'll go and get rid of them immediately! *(Begins to go but adds helplessly)* That's if we can find them! *(Exits)*

F. P.:   Gee, I'm sorry, Saint, I can't think how that happened.

Patrick: *(Being smoothed down by Nennius)* Neither can I, young man. I beg your pardon, but that snake nonsense does get under my beard. As far as I'm concerned there never were any snakes in Ireland, and if there had been, why I should banish them from their native land is more than I could ever understand.

F. P.:   Sure, sure, yeah, I mean... we all understand.

Patrick: Well, I'm glad you do. It seems we have been of some help to you.

F. P.:   Oh, sure! Great! *(Checking clipboard)* Er, just one thing Saint, er... where do the dancing girls come into all this?

Patrick/Nennius: *(Together, shocked)* Girls?!!

F. P.: *(Hurriedly)* Forget it! Forget it! *(Scribbles out girls on list)* No girls. Yeah, yeah, all a mistake, of course, no girls.

Patrick: Well, young man if there is nothing else I can advise you on..?

F. P.: Well, no that's great! You've been a great help! I don't know how we could have managed without you.

Patrick: We were glad to have been of assistance. *(Shakes F. P. by the hand)* If there's nothing more we must be going. Goodbye young man, and may God's blessing rest upon you and your enterprise.

F. P.: Gee, thanks, that's really nice of you. Goodbye Saint, and goodbye Nooni-Nenni- er, so long young fella.

Nennius; Goodbye sir. We look forward to being invited to the premiere. *(They bow and exit Left)*

F. P.: *(Smiling and waving until they go)* Not if I can help it! *(Tucks clipboard under one arm takes out mobile phone and punches number)* Joe? Joe? Get me the casting director – NOW! *(Shouts off stage)* SAM!! *(Into phone)* No, NOW! *(Shouts)* SAM!!

Ass. *(Running in)* Yes, F. P.?

F. P.: Re-instate the snakes!

Ass.: But I thought you said -?

F. P.: Technical advisors! I've had it up to here with technical advisors! Come in here and think they know it all!! Next thing you'll find is they're taking over! *(Into phone)* Right! Now listen, it's Tom Cruise or nobody! *(To Ass.)* What are you waiting for?? *(Ass. runs out)* *(Into phone)* AND GET ME SOME MORE LEPRECHAUNS!!! *(Slams down ariel and storms out.)*

The End

Andrew and the Ancient World

A play for St Andrew's Day
November 30th

Cast:

King Nechthan
Regulus
King Angus
Customs Officer
Andrew
Simon Peter

We know next to nothing about St Andrew apart from the stories in the gospels, and there he is almost totally overshadowed by his brother Simon Peter. All we have to link him with Scotland are his poor bones, but the story of how they came here is historic, if not very edifying. However, Andrew brought his brother to Jesus. How many of us can say the same?

On stage:
At left of stage a vaguely early medieval King/Chief stands with a decorated casket in his hands. This is Nechthan.
At right of stage a similar figure stands also with a casket, this is Angus. He is accompanied by a wild looking monk called St. Regulus.
In the middle of the stage there is the mock up of a small boat with two people in it looking like the illustrations of the disciples in most Bible Story books. These are Simon Peter and Andrew.
The three areas could be illuminated separately as the action takes place.

Nechthan: *(Addressing audience)* This is the year of our Lord 729, and I am Nechthan, King of the Picts in Northern Britain. I am the undoubted ruler of the Scots as well by right of Blood, Conquest and *(Smugly flourishing casket)* by possession of some of the bones of the Holy Saint Peter – himself!

Angus: *(Addressing audience)* I am Angus, <u>rightful</u> king of the Picts and Scots, by right of blood, proposed conquest of the usurper

	Necthan AND *(flourishing his casket)* possession of all the bones of the Blessed Saint Andrew!
Nechthan:	Needless to say, my bones are the real thing, and therefore my claim is under the protection of Saint Peter AND the Pope!
Angus:	My blessed bones are the authentic relics of Saint Andrew, as vouched for by my good friend St. Regulus who carried his precious burden -
Regulus:	*(Smugly)* All the way from CONSTANTINOPLE!
Angus:	ALL the way from Constantinople and therefore my claim is under the protection of the Holy and Blessed Saint Andrew.
Nechthan:	Rumour has it that your pathetic bundle of bones has been lying around collecting dust in Northumbria!
Angus:	*(Opens his mouth to protest, but then turns to Regulus)* Did you come via Northumbria?
Regulus:	Well, I – er - I only stopped at Hexham for Bed and Breakfast.
Angus:	*(Loftily)* Such a rumour is not worth our consideration!
Nechthan:	*(Snarling)* Well, we shall see which of the blessed saints is strongest when it comes to battle!
Angus:	*(Shouting)* Saint Andrew's bones against you AND the pope!
Nechthan:	Saint Peter's relics will destroy you!
Angus:	Usurper!
Nechthan:	Traitor! *(They shake their fists at each other!)*

They stand frozen for a moment and the action switches to the little boat in the middle of the stage. Lighting could be used to emphasise this.
There is a moment of quiet.

Simon is standing in one end of the boat looking ahead, presumably to spot a fish or two. Andrew is at the back steering in a thoughtful manner.

Andrew: Simon?

Simon: Yes?

Andrew: How big is the world?

Simon: *(Turning in surprise)* How should I know? *(Turning back)* Why do you want to know that?

Andrew: Well, it's what He said, you know, "Go into all the world, all the nations"... I mean, well, how many are there?

Simon: *(Shrugs)* Well, I er, I've no idea. I've never really thought about it.

Andrew: Well, I've been doing a lot of thinking. All the world? I mean I've never been further than Jerusalem. *(Gloomily)* And that was a disaster.

Simon: Well, not really, not at the end.

Andrew: I know, but I'm just feeling so – so small, and ignorant. I don't know anything about any other nation.

Simon: *(Turning and sitting down)* Well, let's think about it now. Let's try and count up what we do know. I mean "all the world" must mean the Roman world, mustn't it?

Andrew: And a bit outside, I suppose.

Simon: Yes, but they don't count. *(Doubtfully)* Do they?

Andrew: Well start with us, Palestine, that's one, isn't it?

Simon: And there's Egypt,

Andrew: And Syria,

Simon: Um... er... Cappadocia!

Andrew: That's right, and... and... er Macedonia!

Simon: Of course, there's Italy, Rome itself.

Andrew: But I'm a bit hazy about anywhere after that.

Simon: *(After a moment's thought)* Germanica and – and Gaul!

Andrew: Well, that's good! How do you come to know that?

Simon: I've been talking to Cornelius. These Roman Officers, they get sent all over the place.

Andrew: Yes, a bit like us! Only they get the army to send them. How do we do it?

Simon: Oh, come on now, Andrew, where's your faith? Remember what He said, "I am with you always, even unto the end of the world"!

Andrew: Oh, I know He's with us, but that doesn't buy the tickets, does it?

Simon: The Lord will provide!

Andrew: That's true. But go on, there must be others. I'm sure we've missed one or two.

Simon: Well... I think there's a place called Hispania, and -

Andrew: Crete!

Simon: And Cyprus!

Andrew: And... and... er

Simon:	Er... um...

Andrew: Didn't Cornelius mention anywhere else?

Simon: Well, he did talk about some land beyond the Empire, right to the north. Ultima Thule he called it. That means the very edge of the world!

Andrew: Wow! How do they know? Has anyone ever been there?

Simon: I think so. Cornelius knew some of the legions had been to an island called, er... called um... Bitten, no er... Tannia something... Oh, I can't remember. But it's a terrible place. They're all wild men there, dreadful barbarians, and they paint themselves blue!

Andrew: Oh. *(After a thoughtful pause)* Do you think we're supposed to go there as well?

Simon: I don't know. What do you think?

Andrew: He did say "all nations". Do you think they're a nation?

Simon: *(After a pause)* Er, I'll see what Cornelius has to say about it. *(Stands up again and looks out. They freeze)*

The action switches back to Angus and St. Regulus.

Angus: Right! With St Andrew on our side, now is the time to oust the usurper Nechthan and take my rightful place as King of the Picts and Scots!

Regulus: And may the blessing of Holy Mother Church go with you!

Angus marches to front of stage carrying casket.
Regulus comes behind, supportively.
They are met by a customs official and stopped. This could be a different actor, or Nechthan with an official hat on.

Customs: Right! Just stop there will you.

On entering the kingdom of the Picts and the Scots all aliens must go through customs.

Angus: Aliens? *(Looking at Regulus)* Oh, very well. Just get on with it.

Customs: As you wish sir. Now, purpose of visit?

Angus: Conquest. *(Official writes it on clipboard)*

Customs: I see. Any personal baggage?

Angus: Yes, one army of approximately 20,000 men.

Customs: *(Slowly as he writes it down)* One... army... 20,000.
Well anything else to declare?

Angus: *(Airily)* No, no!

Customs: *(Tapping the casket)* What do you happen to have in this box sir? Could we just take a peek at it?

Angus: *(Proudly)* Ah, now this cask-

Customs: Only we've had a spate of illegal possession of saints' bones!

Angus: AH!! *(Whips round and gives box to Regulus)* Why, this is nothing... er... just one or two knick knacks you know, a few er... souvenirs... er... *(Tries to spread out arms and cloak to cover box. Regulus desperately tries to hide it up his skirts, behind his back.)*

Customs: Yes, we've had a lot of trouble recently. Any number of people trying to smuggle in sacred bones and other relics, especially from the Middle East. Why they say there's not a saint's bone left in Constantinople, not even a little toe!

Angus: Really? How shocking! I – er - I assure you, Officer, we have nothing like that! It's just... er... personal you know... it's a present... that's right, a present!

Customs: What sort of a present, Sir?

Angus: *(Thinking fast)* Well, now that's just it! Er, I wouldn't like to make any mistake about what I am allowed to bring in. Do you think you could just check up on the regulations – you know, get me a list of the duty free?

Customs: Certainly Sir. *(Walks over to left)*

Angus: *(Taking Regulus to one side and whispering loudly and urgently)* Now listen! This is all Nechthan's doing! The dirty dog thinks he can deprive me of the protection of St. Andrew AND lock us up out of the way!

Regulus: *(Wailing)* What can we do?

Angus: Pull yourself together! Listen carefully. I'll keep him talking and you slip out and make for the coast.

Regulus: I'm not going all the way back to Constantinople!

Angus: You won't have to! Just get up to Tayside, find a remote spot on the coast and bury the bones.

Regulus: That's not very respectful!

Angus: Well, build a shrine over it and call it St Andrew's! Only keep a low profile until I've won! *(Regulus hovers about)*

Angus: Well, what are you waiting for? Get going!

Regulus: *(Craftily)* What's in it for me?

Angus: *(Exasperated)* Oh! I - er - er - er how about Bishop? I'll make you a Bishop! And - and I'll build you a golf course!

Regulus: Done! *(Scuttles out right as Customs official returns)*

Angus: Ah, my good man. May I say how impressed I am with the commitment you show to your job. Well done!

Customs: Oh, thank you, sir.

Angus: *(Putting an arm around his shoulders and leading him off left.)* You know I shouldn't be surprised if the new administration wouldn't have a place for a conscientious fellow like you, only something a little more worthy of you.

Customs: That's very kind of you sir! I've always fancied something in the Ministry of Agriculture and Fisheries, with a nice little office in Glasgow.

Angus: Come the victory over Nechthan and the job is yours! *(They exit).*

Back in the boat, Simon moves, still looking for signs of fish.

Andrew: And another thing!

Simon: Now what? *(Turning round).*

Andrew: I've been thinking.

Simon: You're such a worrier, Andrew! What is it now?

Andrew: Well, I don't think I'm cut out for all this preaching lark.

Simon: How do you make that out?

Andrew: I wouldn't be able to think of anything to say! The right words just don't seem to come.

Simon: *(Exasperated)* Andrew! Have I got to remind you again? What did He say? "Take no thought of what you will say, it will be given to you!" And haven't we proved it? Look how we stood up to the High Priest?

Andrew: You did! You and John. I wasn't there, I was outside, knees knocking in the crowd. You know what I'm like in a fight!

Simon:	Nonsense! You're as brave as any man! You'd die for Him, wouldn't you?
Andrew:	That would be easier than standing up before a crowd of thousands the way you did at Pentecost! You were fantastic that day! I couldn't do that in a month of Sundays! Sometimes I get tongue-tied just ordering the milk.
Simon:	*(Soberly)* That wasn't me, Andrew, you know that was the power of the Holy Spirit. I was nothing but a big mouth before I was baptised in the Spirit.
Andrew:	But you always seemed to have something to say.
Simon:	*(Bitterly)* Even if it was to lie that I knew Him.
Andrew:	Oh, Simon, I didn't mean to –
Simon:	It's alright. It's good that I remember. Then I know when I'm preaching the gospel it isn't me, but the power of God.
Andrew:	Well, you've done such a good job up to now!
Simon:	And if I have, who started me off?
Andrew:	What do you mean?
Simon:	Who brought me to Him?
Andrew:	*(Nonplussed)* Oh!… Well, that was nothing really…
Simon:	Nothing? You were the first to recognise Him! Didn't you come to me and say, "We've found the Messiah, the Christ!" when everyone else thought he was just another miracle worker? And you didn't rest until you'd taken me to Him.
Andrew:	*(Bows his head and is silent for a time).*
Simon:	And that's just what you'll go on doing, bringing others to meet Him. I don't know how, and neither do you, but you'll go

wherever He leads you and you'll find the right words to say, and they'll believe you because they'll know, they'll recognise, that you've been with Jesus and you <u>knew</u> Him.

Andrew: *(Silent again for a long moment, then after taking a long, deep breath...)* Okay... Cappodiocia here I come!

Simon: That's my boy! Cappodocia, Egypt, Asia, the far East, the far West! Why, they'll hear you in Ultima Thule!

Andrew: Don't get carried away, Simon! I draw the line at Bitten, whatever it's called, and their hairy barbarians! That's a bit too far. They'd have to <u>carry</u> me <u>there</u>! *(Stands up and looking out)* Hey! You're slipping Simon! Look at all those fish! There must be thousands of them! Get the nets!

Simon: *(Miming throwing the nets over the side)* Here, what does this remind you of?

Andrew: Yeah! And we needed help then! *(Shouting over his shoulder)* Hey! Johnnie! Jimmie! Over here! Quickly! What? *(Listens)* No, I'm not mucking about! It <u>is</u> another miraculous shoal!! *(Both freeze)*

Lights out if used.

The End.

MOORLEY'S

We are growing publishers, adding several new titles to our list each year. We also undertake private publications and commissioned works.

Our range of publications includes:

Books of Verse:
Devotional Poetry
Recitations

Drama
Bible Plays
Sketches
Nativity Plays
Passiontide Plays
Easter Plays
Demonstrations

Resource Books
Assembly Material
Songs and Musicals
Children's Addresses
Prayers and Graces
Daily Readings
Books for Speakers

Activity Books
Quizzes
Puzzles
Painting Books

Church Stationery
Notice Books
Cradle Rolls
Hymn Board Numbers

Please send a stamped addressed envelope (approx. 9" x 6") for the current catalogue or consult your local Christian Bookshop who should stock or be able to order our titles.